More Than Meets The Eye

by

Sandra Williams

MOORLEY'S Print & Publishing

British Library Cataloguing in Publication Data.
A catalogue record for this book is available
from the British Library

ISBN 0 86071 531 0

MOORLEY'S Print & Publishing
23 Park Rd., Ilkeston, Derbys DE7 5DA
Tel/Fax: (0115) 932 0643

2

FOREWORD

However much I try to hide it, my friends always know when I find something amusing. After a recent Sunday morning Service someone asked me what had amused me during the singing of "Tell me the old, old story". I told her that I'd never noticed before that the hymn contained a brilliant name for a firm of Undertakers:

"Tell me the story softly, with
EARNEST TONES AND GRAVE".

She then went on to say that she hoped I never died in suspicious circumstances because she hated to think what they would find if they had to perform a postmortem on my brain.

I do sometimes have daft thoughts but I hope I'm not alone.

Don't you ever wish you could have been an onlooker at the time of Jesus and maybe followed some of the people home to see how their lives were changed?

Wouldn't you like to know who paid for repairs to the roof of the house which was damaged in order to get a sick man to Jesus?

Haven't you ever wondered what kind of childhood Zacchaeus had?

Did the children who sat on Jesus' knee remember when they grew up?

No? Oh dear, I hope I never die in suspicious circumstances!

Sandra Williams

Contents

Lily

Consider the lilies of the field... Solomon in all his glory was not arrayed like one of these (Matthew 6:28-30)

I'm gorgeous, I just know I am
Well, take a look and see
Of all the flowers of the field
Jesus picked out **ME!**

I hadn't always a big head
'Til Jesus once made mention
Of my beauty, to the chagrin
Of that snooty pale blue gentian.

See that foxglove over there?
How can she compete
With a beauty such as mine?
She's clumsy, I'm petite.

The buttercups with yellow skirts
And poppies who are gaudy
All think they're someone in this field
But I think they are tawdry.

———

Mum took me on one side today
And said she'd like a word
"What's this I've been hearing from the weeds?
It's time the truth you heard.

You, my girl, I'm sad to say
Are turning out too vain
Jesus has no favourites
He loves us all the same.

Now I don't mean to belittle you
But it's a mother's duty
To tell you that big head of yours
Detracts somewhat from your beauty."

Mum really gave me a telling off
She said my views are narrow
Instead of choosing a peacock
Jesus talked of the humble sparrow.

I thought of what my mum said
While she prepared our lunch
I suppose flowers **are** much better
When arranged in a mixed bunch.

For of Such is the Kingdom of God

(Mark 10:13-16)
I have a boy of eighteen months
And a girl of almost three
I never will forget the day
Jesus took them on His knee.

His disciples tried to turn them back
But Jesus said "Let them through
Heaven is for such as these
Not just the likes of you."

The love for them upon His face
Is something I'll always remember
A man of strength, a busy life
And yet to them most tender.

When they are grown what shall I say
To make them comprehend
That when they were but children
Jesus treated them as friends?

The Woman at the Well

(John 4:1-42)
I have no husband of my own
And have to make a living
But the women of this town
Are very unforgiving
As I pass they whisper
And then avert their eyes
It's not worth my while to speak to them
For I'll not get a reply.

I admit I am no angel
But it's a lonely life
I'd give anything to swap my status
For that of normal wife.
I see them in the cool of day
Set off to draw their water
I'm not allowed to go with them
They think I'm the devil's daughter.

I have to go at mid-day
When everyone's at ease
That way no-one will shrink from me
As if I were diseased.
Today I went as usual
Water pot upon my head
A stranger was sitting at the well
And this is what He said:

"My friends have gone to the nearby town
To try to buy some food
If I asked you for a drink
Would you think me very rude?"
"But you're a Jew," I said to Him
"And I am from Samaria
You know as well as I do
There's no love lost between each area."

He said to me "Give me a drink
And in return for your endeavour
I will give you living water
And you will live forever."
I don't know why, but I trusted Him
And as we talked some more
He told me all about my life
And He really knew the score.

He knew I'd had five husbands
And was now living in sin
It was pointless trying to hoodwink Him
I somehow knew I wouldn't win
And as we talked I forgot the time
But then His friends came back
They were surprised to see me there
So I hared off down the track.

As I entered the town I felt no fear
For I was too excited
"I've met a man at the Sychar well
And you are all invited...
So come with me and meet Him
He knows all I've ever done
I'm sure that I have met today
A man who is God's son."

I don't know why they believed me
There must have been something in my face
Whatever it was they came with me
To see what had taken place.
And when they had all met Him
They invited Him to stay
He spent two days in our small town
And taught us how to pray.

My life has changed since meeting Him
I've now become accepted
The days long gone before Jesus came
When I always seemed dejected
And if this can happen to the likes of me
Who's never been much good
No-one's beyond redemption
The proof is in the pud.

I've made some friends and now I go
With them to the well at dawn
No more hiding from their eyes
I really feel re-born
So don't ever think you're not good enough
To befriend the Son of Man
I would have thought that at one time
Now I'm His biggest fan!

The Widow's Mite

(Luke 21:1-4)
The woman crept into the Temple
Hoping she wouldn't be seen
Her offering for Temple funds
Compared with others seemed so mean.

But Jesus saw and knew the cost
Of the offering she had made
How much love was in the gift
Given in secret, not displayed.

He knew how poor her life must seem
To those milling all around
But Jesus knew of all of them
Her riches knew no bound.

Others there might flaunt their wealth
As they came to give their tithes
But to Jesus the woman's love
Came as no surprise.

As we go our daily round
The good we do in stealth
Will one day be all repaid
When we inherit Heaven's wealth.

The Colt's Tale

(Mark 11:1-11)
Another long, hot, boring day
Stretches out before me
In this barren landscape
Not very much to see.

Nothing much to do round here
I occasionally stamp my feet
I haven't got much energy
In this Judean heat.

Now and then I rouse myself
And try to swat some flies
The dratted things get everywhere
In nose, and mouth and eyes.

No-one has tried to ride me yet
I'd like to see them try
It would give me such a laugh
To see a grown man cry.

Hello, who's that coming up the road?
I hope it's not some prat
Who thinks he'll make me do some work
'Cos I'm having none of that!

What on earth do they think they're doing?
They're unfastening my rope
I don't want to go with them
I don't think I could cope.

Thank goodness, I'm safe after all
My owner has noticed the men
"What do you think you're doing with him?"
He shouts, and I think I'll count to ten...

His temper is legendary
I expect he will explode
But a quiet word and here I am
Being taken down the road.

Hold on, things are beginning to look up
There are people milling all around
They are starting to put their cloaks on me
I'm deafened by the sound...

People shouting, clapping, cheering
What's happening is a mystery
And then I know what I must do
I must take my place in history.

A man climbs up onto my back
And pats me on the neck
I feel myself puff up with pride
I'll not toss **this** one on the deck.

I feel so important
As I hear some people say
There was once a prophecy
He would enter town this way.

Not on a horse of Arab stock
Caparisoned in gold
But on a humble donkey
Whose tale will oft be told.

The Bible has its Prophets
Its Genesis and Psalms
But the story people like the most
Is the one about the palms...

When people laid them at my feet
And the stony path was smoothed
Not even the hardest of all hearts
Could fail but to be moved.

———

The years have passed, they come and go
But I am never bored
I have my memories of that day
When by all I was adored.

I'm the most famous colt in all the world
Now put out to graze
And I ignore those dratted flies
As I re-live my day of days.

The Observant Wedding Guest

(John 2:1-10)

It's said everyone loves a wedding
And I am no exception
I was invited to one recently
And what I'll tell you is no deception.

The bride looked lovely, the groom was smart
Their faces with love were glowing
The guests were happy, with plenty of food
And wine, like water flowing.

No-one got drunk, our wives saw to that
(I swear mine has eyes like a hawk)
But I noticed concern in the eyes of the hosts
As they gathered together to talk.

It seems they'd miscalculated the wine they would need
And were beginning to feel quite embarrassed
The Steward could see there was none left to serve
And was looking decidedly harassed.

A woman quite near me was watching as well
And saw that the hosts were in trouble
She turned to a man standing talking with friends
Her son? Must be – He's her double.

I heard her whisper "The wine has run out."
Her son looked most ill at ease
"My hour has not come yet," I heard Him exclaim
But His mother just looked and said "Please."

She told all the servants to obey His commands
And He told them to fill to the brim
Some jars standing near them, with water;
They did so, and brought them to Him.

He told them to draw some and take to the Steward
Who could see his job slipping away
I swear to you what happened next
Really made his day.

He lifted the cup to taste what they'd brought
And tasted again, with eyes shining
"The best wine is usually served first," he proclaimed
"But to find wine like this, Oh what timing."

Not many noticed what He had done
Just the servants, His friends and me
And also His mother, who gave Him a smile
Her love and her pride I could see.

When we got home I told the wife
What I'd seen that day
You should have seen the look I got
As she pushed me out of her way.

"That's the last wedding I go to with you
If you can't lay off the drink
How can I go to the shops any more
What will the other wives think?"

I'll never hear the last of it
But I know what I saw
I could do with another miracle
To seize up my wife's jaw.

Whenever we go to weddings now
She watches from across the room
"Don't do it lad," I sometimes feel
Like shouting at the groom.

But then I suppose it does sound daft
To hear this tale of mine
Who in their right mind **would** believe
I saw water turned to wine.

A Nice Way to be "Let Down" by Friends

(Mark 2:1-12)
I never had a head for heights
But I overcame my fear
When I heard that Jesus was in town
In a house not far from here.

Imagine what the owners felt
When my friends made a hole in their roof
I bet they'd always thought before
Their house was burglar-proof.

What else were we supposed to do?
I had to get to Him
Half the town was in that house
They heard nothing for the din.

Anyway, Jesus healed me
Everyone was full of smiles
I'm pleased I can now go to work
As I have to buy some tiles!

The Audition

When they saw the star they rejoiced with exceeding great joy.
(Matthew 2:10)

I live in the heavens with millions of stars
And planets like Pluto, Venus and Mars
People look up at us, we sparkle and glow
As darkness descends we put on quite a show
There are so many of us we're way beyond counting
But here in my galaxy excitement was mounting
We'd heard from a comet that God had a mission
So I decided I'd go and attend the audition.

I arrived at the venue a little unsure
Maybe my talents were, after all, poor
I looked round the room and surveyed all the others
There were sunbeams and moonbeams, along with their mothers
There were comets displaying their long trails of fire
And stars who could twinkle to their hearts desire
I saw shooting stars whose speed was phenomenal
I felt butterflies dancing in a region abdominal.

I started to leave, obviously talent I lack
I made for the door, but a hand held me back
"We haven't yet found what we're looking for
You might just regret it if you walk through that door."
"But I feel inferior in the face of such skill
Just watching those asteroids made me feel ill
I haven't the talent to match any of these
So release my arm and let me go please."

"Now, how do you know you're not just what we need?
There is a job and God has decreed
We have to find someone with the right frame of mind
To help to send a message to the whole of mankind
We have to show all the people on earth
That God's chosen woman is about to give birth
So, what is your talent? You may be just fine
What's your speciality?" – "Me? Oh I just shine."

17

"You're just what we're looking for," he said with a smile
"Oh, I know all the others can put on the style
I've seen them all, put them through their paces
But I can't be doing with miserable faces
As soon as I saw you I knew you were the one
Who could guide those below to God's new-born son
However, I need you to begin right away
Wise men are waiting to start out today."

From my vantage point I saw wonderful things
(I honestly thought Saturn would burst out of her rings)
There were shepherds on a hillside at dead of night
Almost blinded by me when I turned on my light
I guided them, as well I was able
Right to the door of a lowly stable
I helped the Wise Men to fulfil their quest
And when each morning came I laid down for a rest.

I'm quite a celebrity up here in space
And I still watch over the whole human race
You'd be surprised what I see from up here
God's gift of His Son cost Him very dear
I wish sometimes people would open their eyes
Stop what they're doing and look up to the skies
I'm still up here, you'll not hear me whining
For to all the young stars I give lessons in shining.

———

When God has a task for you, please don't succumb
And use others' talents as your rule of thumb
If the job's meant for you, then you are the one
Chosen to lead someone to God's crucified son
We all have our talents, some more than others
But when working for Christ we're all sisters and brothers
If to win souls for Him is your ambition
There is no need to attend an audition
Whoever you are, it isn't a crime
So get out into the world and let your faith shine!

The Web Site

She wrapped him in swaddling clothes,
and laid him in a manger
because there was no room for them in the inn.
(Luke 2:7)

Some of my friends, when settling down
Looked at properties all over town
They wanted to live the suburban dream
And were looking for houses spotlessly clean
They thought me mad when I said I must
Try to find somewhere covered in dust
"Why would you want to live somewhere like that
When you could be comfy in a nice warm flat?"

I'd heard horror stories from other spiders
Who'd spun their webs in fancy houses
The number of times they'd had to rebuild
Because some eager housewife with duster was skilled
What I'm looking for is somewhere quiet
With plenty of flies – (I'm not on a diet)
Then I found it, away from danger
A lovely dark corner over a manger.

I spun my web of intricate lace
Undisturbed, at my own pace
And just when I'd finished and curled up inside
The door of the stable was flung open wide
I heard a voice say "You have my word
If you want to stay here you won't be disturbed
Your wife looks as though her time is near
You'll find nowhere else – I'd settle in here."

I really am grateful," the young man said
"I'll use some of this straw to make her a bed."
The woman just stood there, tired and weary
And glanced round the stable, dingy and dreary
She then said "Joseph, I don't want you to worry
But I think the baby is in a hurry
It's not a palace, but it must be the site
God has chosen for the birth tonight."

The child was born, a baby boy
The couple's faces beamed with joy
I ventured down my silken skein
For a closer look – I remained unseen
I never imagined I could be so beguiled
Just looking into the face of a new-born child
Then I heard people coming, so I scurried away
To witness what happened on that first Christmas Day.

The Innkeeper's wife arrived with the dawn
Surprised to see the baby born
Then shepherds came, they were amazed
At what they'd seen while their sheep grazed
Then the most incredible thing
In through the door walked a real live king
My bottom jaw dropped down to my toes
When two more entered, in marvellous clothes.

They brought gifts from far-off lands
And placed them into Mary's hands
Symbolic gifts of myrrh and gold
And frankincense; their wealth untold
As each one approached her, Mary smiled
As she displayed her lovely child
When at long last they were left alone
She said: "I will be glad when we're back home."

I went to visit my friends in town
Their web's in a house of great renown
They sneered at me and where I live
But I don't care, I can forgive
I tried to tell them I'd seen kings
And angels – real ones – ones with wings
But I couldn't convince them that my humble abode
Was used as the birthplace of the Son of God.

So I left my friends, I didn't pass muster
But I did pass a woman with a feather duster!!

If

If he had been able to live up to the name
Jesus gave him of Peter "The Rock"
His name wouldn't now be synonymous
With the sound of the crow of a cock.

If Only

"If only" are the saddest words
That anyone can say
Especially if they're said to God
At His throne on Judgement Day.

If only you'll forgive me
For my apathy and neglect
I promise for eternity
I'll be forever in your debt.

Only If

We all have heard the warnings
That this day will surely come
And we will be with Him forever
Only if we've loved His son.

Even the Hairs of our Head are Numbered
God knows the hairs upon our head
Whether saint or sinner
Some have got a lot to count
Some are easy, like Yul Brynner.

Zacchaeus

(Luke 19:1-10)
I've always been a little chap,
I just never seemed to grow,
My mother used to shake her head
And say "Eh, I don't know,
I wonder what we'll do with you
If you don't grow to be tall,
The lads around the village
Will pick on someone small."

I grew to be quite devious
I had to, to survive,
Not many people liked me
'Cos I schemed and tricked and lied.
I pretended that I didn't mind
But deep inside it hurt,
But I would never let them know,
So my manner was always curt.

Came the time I had to work
What on earth was I to do?
Jobs for men as small as me
Were far between and few.
I had a lot of interviews
Until the right job came,
I quickly got right to the top
And earned myself a name.

My job was taking cash from folks
In the form of tax and tithe
If a family should have paid, say, three
I always charged them five.
It didn't really bother me
All my workmates did it
Just sometimes in the dead of night
I would worry for a minute.

Rumours were rife in Jericho
About a famous teacher,
It was said he healed the sick and lame
And was also a good preacher.
I heard it said he was on his way
And would pass right through our town,
The crowds were large, no chance for me
To see from so far down.

I spied a tree, the leaves were dense
I could hide without them knowing,
I was always blessed with common sense
It made up for me not growing.
But Jesus stopped right under me
As I peeped out through the branches
"Come down, Zacchaeus," He said,
"There's no need to be anxious."

How did he know my name? I thought
Because I had never met him,
But down I came, with burning face
And waited for some cretin
To laugh at me, to scorn and scoff,
But Jesus didn't despise me,
"Come on," he said, "I need a drink,
Let's go and have some tea."

I realised that day my life
Had not been worth the living
But with Jesus' help I made new friends
Who proved to be forgiving.
I know now that worldly things
Come at too great a cost,
As Jesus said, "The Son of Man
Came to seek and save the lost."

A Father's Love

(Mark 5:21-43)

Jairus had a daughter, she was his pride and joy,
It never crossed his mind to wish she had been born a boy.
She was the apple of his eye, He loved to watch her play,
Her life seemed full of sunshine, until that fateful day.

She seemed to go downhill so fast once the illness struck,
Her mother was beside herself, when Jairus said "Now look,
I know this is a long shot, but Jesus is in town,
I'll see if I can find Him and ask if He'll come round."

"Don't hang about," his wife said, "I don't think she'll last long."
So like a greyhound Jairus ran and pushed right through the throng.
Jairus knelt at Jesus' feet, a father in despair,
Jesus couldn't but be moved by a father's care.

Jairus babbled out his story of how his child was sick,
He asked Jesus to accompany him and said He must be quick.
The crowd could sense a miracle and wouldn't be deterred,
They pushed and shoved and jostled so they could hear every word.

A delay occurred whilst on the way; a woman touched Jesus's cloak
As Jesus stopped to talk to her, Jairus thought that he would choke
Frustration overwhelmed him, he felt like committing a crime,
His daughter's life was running out as Jesus wasted time.

Then someone came to look for him and said "Your child is dead,
Don't bother Jesus any more, your wife needs you instead."
But Jesus heard the message and said "Be not afraid,
If you will only trust in me I'll see that she is saved."

He told the crowds to stay away and chose Peter, James and John
To go with Him and Jairus to see what could be done.
As they approached the house they heard the sound of weeping,
People thought that He had gone mad when Jesus said "She's sleeping...

She is not dead, I'll go to her" and He held her by the hand
"Little girl, get up and walk, come on, I'll help you stand."
The mourners who still wailed outside truly were amazed
When they saw that Jairus' daughter from death to life was raised.

An Old Man's Memories

(John 6:5-15)
One day, as a lad, I decided to go fishing,
While I packed up my gear, my mam in the kitchen
Prepared me some sandwiches of brown bread and tuna,
"Listen now – be home about 5 – preferably sooner."

I set off with my mates to go down to the river,
When folks started passing us, all in a dither.
"Where do you think they're all going?" one of my mates said,
So we decided to follow and see where they led.

We walked quite a way and saw a crowd gathered,
The sun was so hot we all felt quite lathered,
So we sat on the ground to see what would happen,
Then this fellow stood up and all the folks started clapping.

He talked about God and the Kingdom of Heaven,
I looked at my watch, it was half past eleven.
We listened some more, it was rivetting stuff,
Then my belly started rumbling – enough is enough!

I took out my sandwiches – it was hours beyond noon,
Then a woman close by me fell down in a swoon.
All the grown ups said she must have been hungry,
But nobody had brought any food – only me.

The man's friends saw me then, with first sandwich poised,
They said to the man: "Look Sir, one of these boys
Has food in his knapsack, do think you could use it?"
I wasn't too happy, but just had to lose it.

The man who'd been talking didn't half stun us
My sarnies fed me and five thousand others.
I couldn't believe it, I thought I was dreaming,
Then when I got home my mam started screaming...

"I told you this morning you hadn't to be late,
Your dinner's in the oven, shrivelled up on a plate.
You do tell tall stories, you're full of excuses,
You take after your dad – you've not many uses."

"But mam, it is true – I know lying's a sin."
She was just going to clout me when a neighbour came in,
"Eh Jessie, where were you today, were you 'off it'?
We've all seen this fellow – we're sure he's a prophet."

My mam went to hear him the very next day,
Her face was a picture when she heard what he'd to say.
She turned to me: "Oh, our young Rod
Unless I'm mistaken, that man's t'Son of God."

Who Is My Neighbour?
(Luke 10:29-37)

When reading the papers in this day and age
We often find that page after page
Is full of stories of muggings and theft
And people and families who are bereft.
People seem cruel, harsh and unkind,
Youngsters on drugs, stoned out of their mind,
But a headline on Monday made me stop and think
About one man's experience on his way out for a drink.

Apparently, this man was on the A5
When a man filled with road rage left him barely alive.
He was left at the roadside, battered and bleeding,
Hoping someone would give him the help he was needing.
Traffic slowed down and faces peered out
No-one willing to stop at his shout.
Surely someone would help, he thought as he fainted,
But everyone passed by as if he was tainted.

A 'flash' car slowed down and a man in a collar
Looked out of the window and gave a great swallow,
He was, after all, a man of the cloth
And should have been full of compassion and wrath.
But he was a coward and found an excuse
As to why he wouldn't have been of much use.
You see, he'd a meeting in a nearby village
To discuss how Christians could clean up their image.

So, conscience appeased, he put his foot down,
Turned off at the next junction and headed for town,
Got to his meeting with minutes to spare
And took out the notes he'd taken weeks to prepare.
He stood on the platform and puffed out his chest,
Looked out at the audience he hoped to impress,
Then began his lecture and, oh, what a theme,
"How can the Church help the unclean?"

A Churchwarden driving his Volvo Estate
Wonders why the hold-up, he doesn't want to be late,
He's going to the Town Hall, he's receiving a 'gong'
For his work with the victims of those who've done wrong.

He saw the man then, at the side of the road,
By now his temper's all set to explode.
Can't risk stopping and getting himself dirty,
He's expected at the ceremony which starts at 8.30.

Further back in the traffic, radio blaring
Was a Mini with driver who proved to be caring.
The lad who was driving was enormous and black
With earrings and dreadlocks halfway down his back.
"Hey man, what's this?" he said to himself
As he got his first aid kit from the parcel shelf.
He bandaged the man, got him into his car
And took him to a hotel, which wasn't too far.

He booked him into a room and sat up half the night
Until he was sure that the man was alright.
Next morning, as the victim lay sleeping
Down into the lobby our hero went creeping.
The girl at Reception was tired and yawning,
She jumped out of her skin when she heard "Good morning.
I'll square up my bill, I must be away,
Mustn't be late, I get married today.

The chap in Room 20 isn't feeling too good,
 I was wondering if maybe somebody could
Keep popping in to see he's OK.
And I'll see them alright when I come back this way.
I think he's OK now, though he's had quite a shock,
He didn't sleep much, until 5 o'clock
Even then he was restless, his mind in a fog,
He kept mumbling something about men of God."

As I put down the paper I smiled to myself
Went to look for my Bible on the bookshelf.
Hadn't I heard all this once before?
And through the Good Book I started to pore.
Sure enough, there it was, a tale often told
About a man of Samaria in days of old,
A story as told by my precious Saviour,
But 2,000 years on, who is my neighbour?

The Storm

(Matthew 14:22-33)
I had a scare the other night
I'll tell you all about it,
In fact, it gave me such a fright
I sometimes have to doubt it.

We'd been with Jesus all day long
And all of us were shattered,
He wanted to go and pray alone
Because to Him that mattered.

He told us to get in the boat
And leave Him for a while
We waved to Him and He waved back
With a special little smile.

We'd gone three miles, or maybe four,
When we fishermen grew wary,
The wind blew strong, the waves were high
And all around seemed scary.

I thought I was a brave strong chap
Who it took a lot to frighten,
But, believe me, what occurred that night
Made my complexion lighten.

I've never known a wind so fierce,
Not one of us could sleep,
Then we saw Jesus on the lake
Walking on the deep.

"It can't be Him, it is a ghost,"
One of our number cried.
I didn't utter a single word,
I was too terrified.

When Jesus saw the way we were
He said "It's only me."
"OK," I said, "If that's the truth
I'll walk upon the sea."

Then Jesus said "Alright my friend
Let's see what you are made of,
If you will put your trust in me
There's naught to be afraid of."

I couldn't back out, I had to go,
And I did it, I really did it,
I looked at Jesus as I went,
But only for a minute.

I looked away, I saw the waves,
I felt the storm around me.
I went down, I couldn't breathe,
But Jesus' hand soon found me.

He raised me up and made me safe,
Oh boy, was I relieved,
"You didn't hold on to your faith,"
He said, and He was grieved.

I don't think I'll ever doubt again
Wherever in life I'm put
But, just in case I change my mind,
I'll keep my big mouth shut!

The Prodigal Son – 2000 Years On

Jack the lad said to his dad
"I'm fed up with this life,
I don't want all the boring things
Like a mortgage and a wife

I want to go and do the things
A lad of my age should,
But folks your age and thereabouts
Have never understood...

The needs of lads of my age
Are numerous, so just
Give me some of what you've saved
And you'll not see my heels for dust."

And so his dad said "OK son,
It's not my way to smother,
But eh I'm glad she's dead and gone
'Cos this would have killed your mother."

So off Jack went to t' Continent,
To Spain and Greece and Turkey.
He lived it up, he had some fun
From 21 to 30.

His money went first and then his "friends"
And, last of all, his pride.
"I wonder what they think at home,
I bet they think I've died.

If only they could see me now
Hungry, in filth and squalor.
I can't even send a letter home
I've just spent my last dollar.

I wonder what my dad would say
If I went and rang the bell.
I know if I were in his shoes
I'd tell me to go to hell.

But then, my dad was always kind,
Though I thought him an old codger.
I wonder if he'd take me back
And let me be a lodger."

And so Jack went with shoulders bent
Back to the town he'd rejected.
No-one realised just who he was
He looked so frail and dejected.

His dad was at the garden gate,
He wondered "Who's that coming?"
And when he saw it was his son
He jumped up and started running.

He didn't give Jack the chance to say
The speech he had prepared,
He kissed his son and then stepped back
And stared, and stared, and stared.

His dad was grinning from ear to ear
He couldn't hide his glee.
"Eh son, I'm really glad you're home
Come in, I'll make some tea."

The house was filled for days and days
With friends, and joy and laughter.
Jack loved his dad for all his life
From then and ever after.

This tale is told in modern words
That from it we may learn
God waits and watches all the time
For the prodigals to return.

We only have to say to Him
"Oh Father, please forgive,"
And He will show us evermore
The right, best way to live.

The Stations of the Cross

First Station – Jesus is condemned to death
Pilate was a stupid man
Without much common sense
Anyone but a fool could see
Jesus had committed no offence.
But even as he washed his hands
As if to shed the blame
His conscience must have told him
He would always bear the shame.

Second Station – Jesus is mocked by the soldiers
The soldiers were in a foreign land
Often of home they would dream,
Jesus was just a sitting duck
On whom to vent their spleen.
They spat on Him and struck Him,
Did all manner of dreadful things
They weren't aware that the man they mocked
Was truly the King of Kings.

Third Station – Jesus falls for the first time
Jesus is forced to take up His cross,
The full weight of the beam,
The agony is so intense
It almost makes Him scream.
The road to death has now begun,
Calvary draws nigh
Jesus stumbles to His knees,
The crowd breathes out a sigh.

Fourth Station – Jesus meets his mother
Jesus sees Mary, the mother He loves,
Her face full of sorrow and grief.
The events of this, her son's short life
Seem almost beyond belief.
Jesus knows what she is feeling as He passes by,
How would any mother cope with watching her son die?
But Mary knows it is His fate, what He was born to do,
He had to die upon that cross – for her, for me, for you.

Fifth Station – Simon of Cyrene is compelled to carry the cross
Simon of Cyrene came into the town
And saw this sordid scene
And as he watched he wondered
What could this whole thing mean?
Jesus was tired, he needed some help
And Simon was drawn in
To play his part in history
As Jesus conquered sin.

Sixth Station – Veronica wipes the face of Jesus
Veronica, so legend says,
Was also in the plan.
She it was who mopped the brow
Of the Son of Man.
When later she took out the veil
She'd used to wipe His face,
She saw His imprint was still there,
Which time would not erase.

Seventh Station – Jesus falls the second time
The road is long, the sun beats down,
Satan must be gloating.
Jesus looks around Him
And all he sees is loathing.
The face Veronica had tried to clean
Is now pressed in the ground.
The crowd looks on and wonders
This time will He come round?

Eighth Station – The women of Jerusalem mourn for Jesus
As Jesus walked He heard the crowds
Shouting, mocking, jeering
And then He saw a group of women
And that they were all weeping.
"Daughters of Jerusalem,
Do not cry for me,
But for yourselves and children.
This day is meant to be."

Ninth Station – Jesus falls the third time
It's now mid-day, the sun is high
The heat is hard to bear.
The hill's in sight where He will die
Doesn't anybody care?
He falls again, He cannot stand,
The pain is now past bearing.
And yet again He rises
And sees just faces staring

Tenth Station – Jesus is stripped of his clothes
And the final insult,
Jesus is stripped bare,
His garment taken from Him,
Sewn with loving care.
They drag it from His body
For all the world to see.
His modesty offended,
He keeps His dignity.

Eleventh Station – Jesus is nailed to the cross
Words can't express this Station,
I couldn't if I tried
The best brains of any nation
Can't tell how Jesus died.
In agony he suffered,
The pain was so severe.
This is the man whose love for us
Makes us Him revere.

Twelfth Station – Jesus dies on the cross
Greater love hath no man,
We've often heard it said.
The insults still come thick and fast
As Jesus hangs His head.
"My God, my God," His cry rings out
As death seems to be winning.
Then, "It is finished," His work complete,
But ours is just beginning.

Thirteenth Station – The body of Jesus is taken from the cross
They take Him down but to make sure
A soldier thrusts a spear.
Mary takes possession of her son
And wipes away a tear.
She's glad it is all over,
Her son has been so brave.
The only thing she can do now
Is see Him to His grave.

Fourteenth Station – The body of Jesus is laid in the tomb
Joseph had bought himself a tomb
For when his life should cease
But he gave it up for Jesus
When His body was released.
They left Him there, they said goodbye
And then rolled up the stone
And sadly went their weary way
And left Him all alone.

There is no Fifteenth Station
But the disciples watch and pray
And after that Good Friday
Comes Resurrection Day.
So all that pain and all that grief
And all that He went through
Has to strengthen our belief
It was for me and you.